RECORD BREAKERS
ANIMALS

DANIEL GILPIN

WAYLAND

First published in 2010 by Wayland

Copyright © Wayland 2010

Wayland
338 Euston Road
London NW1 3BH

Wayland Australia
Level 17/207 Kent Street
Sydney NSW 2000

Senior Editor: Debbie Foy
Designer: Rob Walster
Picture Researcher: Kate Lockley

British Library Cataloguing in Publication Data:
Gilpin, Daniel.
   Record breakers.
   Animals.
   1. Animals--Miscellanea--Juvenile literature.
   2. World
   records--Juvenile literature.
   I. Title
   590-dc22

ISBN: 9780750262743

Printed in China

Wayland is a division of
Hachette Children's Books,
an Hachette UK company.

www.hachette.co.uk

Picture credits:

Arco Images GmbH/Alamy: 18
Australia Zoo/Handout/Reuters/Corbis: 28BL
Amanda Balmain/iStockphoto: 2, 6
© Miles Barton/naturepl.com: 22
Brandon Cole Marine Photography/Alamy: 28
© Pete Cairnes/naturepl.com: 12
© Jurgen Freund/naturepl.com: 14-15, 20-21
© Tony Heald/naturepl.com: 26-27
Michio Hoshini/Minden Pictures/FLPA: 25
ImageBroker/Imagebroker/FLPA: 7
Andrejs Jegorovs/iStockphoto: 11, 30
© Steven Kazlowski/naturepl.com: 24
Konstantin Kirillov/iStockphoto: 27TR
Hiroya Minakuchi/Minden Pictures/FLPA: 4-5
© Rolf Nussbaumer/naturepl.com: 19
Jamie Otterstetter/iStockphoto: 9TR
© Doug Perrine/naturepl.com: 13
M Reel/Shutterstock: 28-29
Cyril Ruoso/Minden Pictures/FLPA: Cover, 23
Robert Tyrell/OSF/Photolibrary Group: 16-17
John Warburton-Lee Photography/Alamy: 20C
© Doc White/naturepl.com: 5BR
Winfried Wisniewski/FN/Minden Pictures/FLPA: 10-11
Klaus-Peter Wolf/Imagebroker/FLPA: 8-9
Jeanette Zehentmayer/iStockphoto: 15TR

Abbreviations used:

m = metres
ft = feet
in = inches
km = kilometres
cm = centimetres
mm = millimetres
kg = kilogrammes
lb = pounds

Tricky words are listed in 'But What Does That Mean?' on page 31.

WHAT'S INSIDE?

BLUE WHALE 4

AFRICAN BUSH ELEPHANT 6

GIRAFFE 8

CHEETAH 10

PEREGRINE FALCON 12

COSMOPOLITAN SAILFISH 13

BOX JELLYFISH 14

BEE HUMMINGBIRD 16

COMMON SWIFT 18

DUNG BEETLE 19

WHALE SHARK 20

RETICULATED PYTHON 22

SALTWATER CROCODILE 23

POLAR BEAR 24

OSTRICH 26

GALAPAGOS GIANT TORTOISE 28

TEST YOURSELF! 30

BUT WHAT DOES THAT MEAN? 31

CHECK IT OUT & INDEX 32

BLUE WHALE

The blue whale is the largest animal ever. It can reach 33.5 m (110 ft) long. This is longer than three buses parked end to end!

Can you believe it?

The largest blue whales are so heavy they can weigh even more than a jumbo jet!

On the other hand...

The smallest animals in the world are called mesozoans (MEE-so-ZOE-ans). They are so tiny that they can only be seen with a microscope!

The blue whale breathes through blowholes on the top of its head.

WOW!

THE BLUE WHALE'S HEART IS THE SIZE OF A SMALL FAMILY CAR. ITS BIGGEST BLOOD VESSELS ARE SO WIDE THAT A PERSON COULD SWIM DOWN THEM!

To feed, blue whales filter tiny, shrimp-like creatures called krill.

AFRICAN BUSH ELEPHANT

BIGGEST ON LAND!

The African bush elephant is the world's largest land animal. Large males can weigh as much as 100 men put together! Bush elephants are also very tall. The biggest can be 4 m (13 ft) high at the shoulder!

Elephants drink by sucking up water and squirting it into their mouths.

Can you believe it?

Bush elephants are so strong they can push trees over to get at leaves when other food is hard to find!

WOW!

AN ELEPHANT'S TRUNK CONTAINS AROUND 40,000 MUSCLES!

This male (bull) elephant is much bigger than a female (cow) elephant.

GIRAFFE

TALLEST!

The giraffe is the world's tallest animal. Males are usually bigger than females and can grow up to 6 m (20 ft) tall. This is the same height as a house!

Can you believe it?

Female giraffes give birth standing up. This means that their babies enter the world with a bump – falling nearly 2 m (7 ft) to the ground.

WOW!

THE GIRAFFE'S NECK IS THE LONGEST OF ANY LIVING ANIMAL. EVEN SO, IT ONLY CONTAINS SEVEN BONES – THE SAME NUMBER AS A HUMAN'S!

Giraffes are so tall they must spread their front legs to drink!

A giraffe's tongue is long and muscular. It is used to strip leaves from branches.

CHEETAH

The cheetah can run faster than any other animal. Its top speed is more than 96 km (60 miles) per hour!

Can you believe it?

A cheetah can speed up faster than a Ferrari. This amazing cat goes from 0–97 km (0–60 miles) per hour in just three seconds!

At top speed, a cheetah can cover 8 m (26 ft) with each stride.

WOW!

A CHEETAH'S CLAWS ACT LIKE RUNNING SPIKES, GIVING IT EXTRA GRIP AS IT SPEEDS OVER THE GROUND!

A cheetah and a vulture fight for the same prey.

CONTENDERS

The greatest long-distance runner is the pronghorn antelope from North America. It can run at an amazing 88 km (55 miles) per hour for 0.8 km (0.5 miles)!

PEREGRINE FALCON

The peregrine falcon is the fastest bird on Earth. With its wings folded to dive at prey, it can reach speeds of 200 km (124 miles) per hour!

Can you believe it?

Falcons often nest on ledges or in caves high up on a cliff. Some peregrine falcons have even nested in bridges and skyscrapers.

A peregrine falcon uses its sharp claws and beak to tear its prey apart.

COSMOPOLITAN SAILFISH

The sailfish is the world's fastest swimmer. It lives in the open ocean where it hunts other fast-moving fish.

Can you believe it?

At top speed, the sailfish can reach 109 km (68 miles) per hour. This is over 13 times quicker than the fastest human swimmer!

FASTEST SWIMMER!

WOW!
THE COSMOPOLITAN SAILFISH CAN QUICKLY CHANGE COLOUR TO CONFUSE ITS PREY.

BOX JELLYFISH

The box jellyfish is one of the world's most deadly creatures. One large jellyfish has enough venom to kill 60 people!

Can you believe it?

Box jellyfish often swarm off the coast of Australia and have killed lots of swimmers. Some victims have been stung and died in less than four minutes!

Box jellyfish have transparent bodies, making them hard to spot in the water.

WOW!

BOX JELLYFISH MAY HAVE UP TO 60 TENTACLES TRAILING FROM THEIR BODIES. EACH TENTACLE CAN REACH UP TO 3 M (10 FT) LONG!

Many beaches in Australia have warning signs about box jellyfish!

CONTENDERS

The world's most venomous land animal is the inland taipan from Australia. This snake's venom is 500 times stronger than that of the Indian cobra!

BEE HUMMINGBIRD

The bee hummingbird is the smallest bird in the world. It comes from Cuba in the Caribbean, and is only about 5 cm (2 in) long!

Can you believe it?

The bee hummingbird is so small that it weighs just a little more than a paper clip!

SMALLEST BIRD!

The tiny bee hummingbird is often mistaken for a bumble bee.

The bee hummingbird has a long beak and tongue to push into the centre of flowers and feed on sugary nectar.

The bee hummingbird can hover in one spot like a helicopter!

WOW!

THE BEE HUMMINGBIRD BEATS ITS WINGS AROUND 80 TIMES A SECOND. IT IS SUCH A SKILFUL FLIER THAT IT CAN HOVER – AS WELL AS FLY BACKWARDS!

COMMON SWIFT

The common swift travels further than any other creature. It spends most of its life flying at speed, and only lands to build a nest and raise its chicks.

The common swift flies at speeds of up to 111 km (69 miles) per hour!

Can you believe it?

The common swift flies non-stop for two or three years after fledging. During that time it eats, drinks and even sleeps while flying!

DUNG BEETLE

Dung beetles are the world's strongest animals for their size. Some can pull objects more than 1,000 times their own body weight. This is like an average man pulling six buses!

Can you believe it?

Dung beetles feed on the dung of other animals. Male beetles roll up giant balls of dung to present to females. The females break up the dung balls and lay their eggs in them!

The largest dung beetles can grow to 6 cm (2.5 in).

WHALE SHARK

The world's biggest fish can grow to 18 m (60 ft) long. This is twice as long as a bus – but the whale shark is also three times as heavy!

Can you believe it?

The whale shark feeds by filtering small creatures from the water. It swims along with its mouth open and swallows whatever goes in.

A whale shark's mouth is 1.5 m (5 ft) wide. This is big enough to swallow a person whole!

On the other hand...

The smallest fish in the world is the Indian Ocean dwarf goby. Fully grown, the dwarf goby is less than 9 mm (0.3 in) long!

The whale shark is a gentle giant, and does not pose a danger to divers.

WOW!

ALTHOUGH THEY ARE HUGE, WHALE SHARKS ARE DOCILE FISH AND SOMETIMES ALLOW SWIMMERS TO HITCH A RIDE!

RETICULaTED PYTHuN

The reticulated python is the world's longest snake. It lives wild in south-east Asia and can grow up to 10 m (33 ft) long.

LONGEST SNAKE!

Can you believe it?

The reticulated python suffocates its prey. With each outward breath of its victim, the snake's coils tighten around the prey until it cannot breathe in. It can also dislocate its jaw to swallow large prey!

This reticulated python has dislocated its jaw to allow it to swallow and feed on a deer!

SALTWATER CROCODILE

Saltwater crocodiles are found from India to Australia. They can grow to 7 m (23 ft) long and weigh the same as a small car!

Can you believe it?

Saltwater crocodiles live in coastal rivers, but also swim in the ocean. They have often been spotted way out at sea – far from the nearest land!

WOW!

SALTWATER CROCODILES ARE THOUGHT TO KILL AND EAT 2,000 PEOPLE EVERY YEAR!

POLAR BEAR

The polar bear is the largest meat-eating land animal in the world. Reared up on its back legs, it can reach 3.4 m (11 ft) tall!

Can you believe it?

Large adult males can weigh up to 750 kg (1,600 lb)! But a polar bear's body weight changes through the year, as it can lose a lot of weight during hibernation.

BIGGEST LAND CARNIVORE!

WOW!

POLAR BEARS HAVE AN AMAZING SENSE OF SMELL. THEY CAN PICK UP THE SCENT OF A DEAD SEAL FROM MORE THAN 32 KM (20 MILES) AWAY.

A polar bear rears up at a truck window, as the cameraman snaps a picture!

Believe it or not, a polar bear's skin is black! This helps to soak up the warmth from sunlight. The hairs of its fur are transparent and only look white because of the way light is scattered by the hairs.

OSTRICH

The ostrich is the world's biggest bird. Males can grow up to 2.75 m (9 ft) tall, and can sprint at speeds of 72 km (45 miles) per hour!

Can you believe it?

A kick from an ostrich is so powerful that it could kill a human being or a predator such as a lion!

WOW!

THE NEW ZEALAND MOA WAS EVEN BIGGER THAN THE OSTRICH! THESE GIANT BIRDS STOOD UP TO 4 M (13 FT) TALL, BUT WERE HUNTED SO MUCH THEY DIED OUT ABOUT 600 YEARS AGO.

Ostrich eggs are the world's largest. They weigh 20 times more than hens' eggs.

CONTENDERS

The emu is the world's second largest bird. It can grow to about 1.8 m (6 ft) tall and, like the ostrich, it cannot fly.

Male ostriches will hatch the eggs and look after the young.

GALAPAGOS GIANT TORTOISE

The Galapagos giant tortoise lives longer than any other animal on Earth. Some live to be well over 150 years old!

Can you believe it?

Like all tortoises, these gentle giants do everything slowly. They eat plants and have no natural predators in the wild.

The late Steve Irwin and his wife, Terri, pose with Harriet at Queensland Zoo, Australia.

WOW!

THE OLDEST KNOWN GALAPAGOS GIANT TORTOISE WAS NAMED HARRIET. BROUGHT FROM THE GALAPAGOS ISLANDS IN 1835, HARRIET LIVED TO THE GRAND OLD AGE OF 175!

The Galapagos tortoise may spend up to 16 hours a day sleeping!

TEST YOURSELF!

Can you remember facts about the record-breaking animals in this book? Test yourself here by answering these questions!

1. What is the world's largest fish?

2. What is the world's smallest bird?

3. What is the name of the oldest known Galapagos giant tortoise?

4. What is the world's largest animal?

5. How many bones are there in a giraffe's neck?

6. Which country is home to the inland taipan, the world's most venomous land animal?

7. Where can the world's longest snake be found?

8. True or false? The common swift sleeps while it is in mid-air.

9. Which is faster, an ostrich or a cheetah?

10. What colour is a polar bear's skin?

Answers

1. The whale shark
2. The bee hummingbird
3. Harriet
4. The blue whale
5. Seven
6. Australia
7. South-east Asia
8. True
9. A cheetah
10. Black

BUT WHAT DOES THAT MEAN?

carnivore   A meat-eating animal.

docile   This means gentle, easily handled and not aggressive.

dislocate   To disconnect a joint in the body.

dung   Waste that passes from an animal's body.

falcon   A bird of prey.

filter   To remove small things from a liquid, as you might do with a sieve.

fledging   The process of growing adult feathers and learning to fly.

hibernation   A long and very deep sleep that lasts through the winter.

hover   To stay at the same point in mid-air, while flying.

mesozoan   A very tiny, simple, worm-like animal made up of just a few cells.

microscope   Something that is used to look at small objects.

nectar   A sweet, sugary liquid that is made by flowers to attract insects and other creatures.

predator   An animal that kills other animals for food.

prey   Animals that are killed and eaten by predators.

reptile   An animal that breathes air and has dry, scaly skin.

skyscraper   A very tall building with lots of floors.

species   This is a particular type of animal or plant. Male and female members of the same species can mate to produce young.

suffocate   To choke or kill by stopping the victim from breathing.

swarm   When animals move around in very large numbers.

tentacles   Long 'feelers' that are used for moving or feeling.

transparent   Another word for 'see-through'.

venom   Another word for poison.

CHECK IT OUT & INDEX

Check out these amazing places to go and websites to visit!

London Zoo, England
Britain's best known zoo with over 700 species!

Natural History Museum, London, England
This famous museum features a life-size model of a blue whale.

San Diego Zoo, San Diego, USA
One of the world's most famous zoos.

Australia Zoo, Beerwah, Queensland, Australia
Australia's most famous zoo features the world's most venomous snake.

http://animals.nationalgeographic.com/animals/photos/animal-records-gallery
This website has pictures and information about all sorts of record-breaking animals!

http://www.guinnessworldrecords.com/records/natural_world
The Guinness World Records is the place to find out about other records from the natural world.

http://www.arkive.org
A fantastic website packed with great pictures and information about all sorts of animals!

Index

A
African bush elephant 6–7
age 28

B
babies 8, 18, 27
birds 12, 16–17, 18, 26, 27
blood vessels 5
blue whale 4–5
bones 8

C
cheetah 10–11
colour 13, 14, 25

D
dung beetle 19

F
fish 13, 14–15, 20, 21
food and drink 5, 6, 9, 11, 12, 13, 17, 18, 19, 20, 22, 23, 28

G
Galapagos giant tortoise 28–29
giraffe 8–9

H
heart 5

K
krill 5

M
mesozoans 4
muscles 6, 9

N
nesting 12, 18

P
polar bear 24–25
pronghorn antelope 11

S
saltwater crocodile 23
senses 24
size and weight 4, 5, 6, 7, 8, 9, 15, 16, 19, 20, 22, 23, 24, 26, 27
skin and hair 25
snakes 15, 22
speed 10, 11, 12, 13, 17, 18, 26

V
venom 14, 15

RECORD BREAKERS

Contents of titles in the series:

ANIMALS
9780750262743

Blue Whale
African Bush Elephant
Giraffe
Peregrine Falcon
Cosmopolitan Sailfish
Box Jellyfish
Bee Hummingbird
Common Swift
Dung Beetle
Whale Shark
Reticulated Python
Saltwater Crocodile
Polar Bear
Ostrich
Galapagos Giant Tortoise
Test Yourself!
But What Does That Mean?
Check It Out & Index

CARS
9780750262750

Bugatti Veyron
Hummer H1 Alpha Wagon
Nuna 2
Pagani Zonda
Thrust SSC
Toyota Corolla
Bugatti 'Royale' Type 41
Ultimate Aero TT
VW L1
Dodge Viper SRT–10
Morgan 4/4
Inspiration
Peel P50
Lamborghini Gallardo
Test Yourself!
But What Does That Mean?
Check It Out & Index

BUILDINGS
9780750262774

ADX Florence
Angkor Wat
Boeing Everett factory
Grand Central Terminal
Burj Khalifa
Ice Hotel
Djenne Grand Mosque
May Day Stadium
Rose Tower
Istana Nurul Iman
Screen Room
Cross Island Chapel
The O2
Great Pyramid at Giza
Suurhusen Church
Yokohama Marine Tower
Test Yourself!
But What Does That Mean?
Check It Out & Index

PEOPLE
9780750262767

Mariusz Pudzianowski
Darren Taylor
David Weichenberger
Fred Grzybowski
Christian Schou
Usain Bolt
Thomas Gregory
Herbert Nitsch
Dave Cornthwaite
Ronaldo
Alia Sabur
Ashrita Furman
Jordan Romero
Jeanne L Calment
Mark Zuckerberg
Valeri Polyakov
Test Yourself!
But What Does That Mean?
Check It Out & Index

WAYLAND